ACCELERATE

YOUR

LEADERSHIP

DEVELOPMENT

IN TRAINING

DOMAIN

*Proven Success Strategies for New
Training & Learning Managers*

Raman K. Attri

ISBN 978-981-14-0066-7 (Print book)
ISBN: 978-981-11-8991-3 (e-book)
First published: December 2018
Lead author: Raman K. Attri
Published by Speed To Proficiency Research: S2Pro©
Published at Singapore
Printed in the United States of America

National Library Board, Singapore Cataloguing in Publication Data

Names: Attri, Raman K., 1973-
Title: Accelerate your leadership development in training domain : proven success strategies for new
      training & learning managers / Raman K. Attri.
Description: Singapore : Speed To Proficiency Research, [2018] | Includes bibliographic references.
Identifiers: OCN 1055689439 | ISBN 978-981-14-0066-7 (paperback) |
ISBN 978-981-11-8991-3 (e-book)
Subjects: LCSH: Employee training personnel–Training of. | Employees–Training of.
Classification: DDC 658.3124–dc23

Speed To Proficiency Research: S2Pro©
A research and consulting forum
Singapore 560463
https://www.speedtoproficiency.com
rkattri@speedtoproficiency.com

Over 35 success strategies across 8 strategic competencies

Decision-making, Operations management, Training management, Project leadership, Strategic leadership, Global team leadership, and Professional development

CONTENTS

ABOUT THE BOOK

This book is a comprehensive source of guidance for individual contributors who have just transitioned (or about to transition) to new roles in training domain such as training managers, learning managers or instructional design manager or any such roles to accelerate their leadership in training domain. The book describes S2Pro© Model of Strategic Competencies for Training and Learning Management Function, developed out of years of practice and research, which proposes a framework for accelerating leadership and management development path of new training or learning managers.

The book delivers 35 powerful, proven strategies across 8 core strategic competencies namely thought process, decision-making, operations management, project leadership, strategic leadership, global team leadership, and professional development. The book provides authentic understanding, knowledge, insight, and guidance required to be successful in training domain. This book is the first-of-its-kind focused exclusively on the aspect of accelerating leadership and management development path for new training and learning managers.

Chapter 1 of the book introduces a Model of Strategic Competencies for Training and Learning Function outlining 8 core strategic competencies to accelerate leadership development.

Chapter 2 sets the stage on making 3 changes in one's thought process to be successful in the new role.

Chapter 3 of the book provides insight into 3 core skills required by new training and learning managers to make effective training related decisions.

Chapter 4 of the book equip new managers with an understanding of 3 pillars that would allow them to manage their training operations amidst the complexity of the organization.

Chapter 5 of the book focuses on 2 fundamental characteristics of highly successful training management practices.

Chapter 6 describes 2 powerful project leadership styles particular for leading learning or training related projects.

Chapter 7 shifts its focus on providing the first-of-its-kind checklist of 10 unique approaches exhibited by well-known training leaders.

Chapter 8 then dives into the challenge of team leadership, in particular for global, diverse multi-cultural training teams and describes 3 common-sense principles to handle this challenge.

Chapter 9 concludes the book by providing 5 success strategies to new managers to develop themselves professionally to maintain a competitive edge in what they do.

Chapter 1

STRATEGIC

COMPETENCIES

8 CORE STRATEGIC COMPETENCIES TO ACCELERATE LEADERSHIP DEVELOPMENT

This practice-oriented book is based on extensive experience and research on how the journey of individual contributors in training or learning function can be accelerated tremendously toward a successful management role.

This book is designed around a Model of Strategic Competencies for Training and Learning Function. This model was the outcome of over

10 years of research and practice-based inferences from over 20 years of my experience at various training and learning roles starting from being a trainer, instructional designer, and learning specialists, learning or training consultant to all the way to a senior management role in training and learning function.

At a high level, this model presents the strategic competencies fundamental to success in training and management function. As a note, this model does not focus on day-to-day operational competencies generally covered by other models. However, this model has a particular use in "accelerating" the development path and reducing time to proficiency of individual contributors like trainers, instructors, designers, learning specialists and instructional designers to develop them to take up a management role in the same function.

The model lays out the competencies and over 35 strategies to develop those competencies in targeted individuals. HR practitioners and L&D specialists can use this as a guide to design accelerated leadership development path for brilliant individual contributors. These strategies provide directions in regard to the nature of assignments that build their competencies across 8 strategic areas.

The model covered in this book is based on 8 core strategic competencies required for any training and learning management function:

1. **Thought process**
2. **Decision-making**
3. **Operations management**
4. **Training management**

5. Project leadership
6. Strategic leadership
7. Global team leadership
8. Professional development

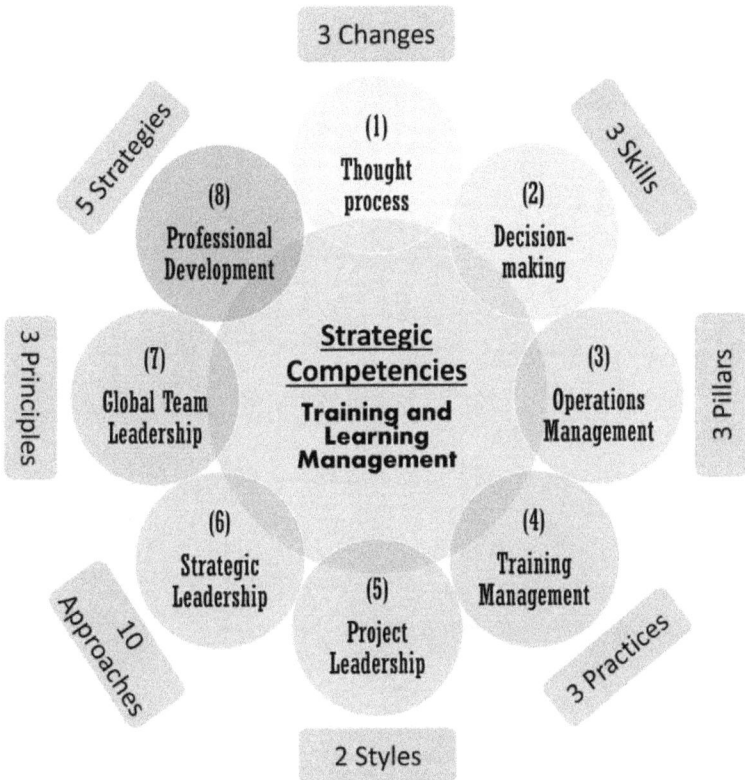

3 Changes

3 Strategies

3 Skills

(8)
Professional
Development

(1)
Thought
process

(2)
Decision-
making

3 Principles

(7)
Global Team
Leadership

**Strategic
Competencies**
**Training and
Learning
Management**

(3)
Operations
Management

3 Pillars

(6)
Strategic
Leadership

(5)
Project
Leadership

(4)
Training
Management

10 Approaches

3 Practices

2 Styles

S2Pro© Model of 8 Strategic Competencies for
Training and Learning Management Function

The model provides guidance with over 35 strategies that can be used to build or develop these competencies.

♦ ♦ ♦ ♦ ♦

Chapter 2

THOUGHT PROCESS

MAKE 3 CHANGES IN YOUR THOUGHT PROCESS FOR SUCCESSFUL TRAINING MANAGER'S ROLE

"Thought Process" is the first strategic competency in S2Pro© model of strategic competencies for training and learning management function for developing new training and learning managers. The thought process that is required in any training and learning function fundamentally makes it different from any comparable function in other streams. S2Pro© model of strategic competencies emphasizes starting with the thought process as opposed to other models which tend to start with skills. The model proposes inducting 3 fundamental changes in the thought process of new training/learning managers.

In general, in any profession, individual contributors tend to quite smoothly move into a manager's role in the same profession if the competencies required at a manager's role is just an extension of competencies employed at a contributor's role. Ironically, I found that training and learning management roles stand at some exception where there is a big leap between the competencies required by management role versus the competencies required in at an individual contributor's role. If you were an individual contributor a while ago and now have taken up the role of a new training/learning manager, then your overall perspective, the thought process, and approaches would need a thorough overhaul.

When you move up to a role of managing the training delivery as opposed to delivering the training itself, your tremendous experience as a trainer, instructional designer or learning professional no doubt will help you get you success in your new role. However, you would need to learn the new game quickly and reorient your thought process and approaches. This chapter describes the three most important changes you need to bring in your thought process and start practicing while you prepare yourself to move up to training or learning management role.

CHANGE #1: CUSTOMER NEEDS - PARTNERSHIP WITH CUSTOMERS TO FIND SOLUTIONS TO MEET CUSTOMER NEEDS

When you step up to training or learning management role, the definition and the spectrum of a customer's needs or expectations expand much beyond training as the only solution. Management of training and learning function is all about keeping a tight focus on customer needs.

Let's think it through two scenarios. Imagine the time when you were a trainer assigned to deliver a training program. Your focus usually used to be on a couple of objectives like:

1. How are you going to deliver information effectively to your 'customer' who is sitting in my training session?
2. How can you make a difference to his skills which helps him to do his job more effectively?

You might have been able to address these two the objectives by using a strategy to understand a customer's needs during the training session. That's a typical way you might have been able to meet customer expectations.

Now let's take the same scenario as a training manager. Let's see how the thought process is going to change the moment you take up the management role:

a) Your focus shifts to finding a variety of solutions to meet a customer's needs, the training being one among many available solutions.
b) The important paradigm shift that happens in this role is to strike a partnership with the customer. The customer may not always need training as a solution. As a partner, you may have to understand the real needs.
c) Your role in training management will become to keep the focus on different solutions possible which can add great value to the customer, increase his satisfaction and enhance future alliance.

In reality, while you were a trainer, someone (usually your training manager) would have already analyzed the fact that delivering a training program indeed was the right solution for a given situation. That's why that customer was attending your training session.

If you are stepping up to a management role, make sure you know that: You main goal would be to find the best solutions. Most customers (internal or external) tend to view training as an important mechanism to solve their problems. However, in reality, training may not be the only solution which a customer might be looking for in a given situation. We have seen that at times we find customers not being able to articulate the real needs and get trapped in their traditional, narrow field of view. Some examples: the customer may have skill retention issue among the staff and not per se the fresh training, or customer may just need to get hold of a well-written procedure as opposed to the theory behind it. Tons of such similar situations form your job scope, and it will require you to expand focus away from thinking that training is the only solution customer may need. I must mention here that this expanded focus is a big challenge for a trainer to adjust quickly while moving up to a training management role. Similarly, the instructional designer stepping up as an instructional design manager may face a challenge how quickly he can understand that designing a course may not always be the first solution, though the job title states the word 'instructional design' in it.

This orientation as a manager, though not very much visible to your direct reports, is instrumental in striking a partnership with the customer and brings more business without actually having to design and deliver a training program. This might sound counterintuitive, but this is how it is.

Remember, as a training manager or instructional design manager or a learning manager, a larger percentage of your analysis, solutions, and recommendations may not even convert into a real training session or an instructional design project ever.

Therefore, start making this important change in your thought process. Now you have a customer having non-training needs too. More quickly you adjust to this paradigm shift in the thought process, more successful you will be in your new role.

CHANGE #2: BUSINESS PRIORITIES - RESPONDING FAST TO CHANGING BUSINESS PRIORITIES

Let's see how you used to view a situation as a trainer:

You are conducting a training session, and it is almost the last day of the tiring training program. You are quite relieved that next week you have a little break off the podium conducting several training sessions in a row. You go home and plan out a nice dinner with your spouse and kids. All of a sudden, some high-pressure situation landed from somewhere that now requires you to conduct another training session next week for a high-value customer away from his home location. Understandably, you probably may not be ready to respond to such a lightning change in priority and your schedule. Quite reasonably you would think that management did not plan the things well for you. You may even think to the extent that your manager was insensitive about your priorities.

This is quite a natural reaction when you are a trainer. By nature of the job, your reaction time to respond to a pressing business priority may be relatively slow. Also, the amount of pressure that comes to you is limited or already filtered through several layers of managerial or stakeholders.

Let us flip this situation around when you step up to a training management role:

Now, your job is staying in business and responding fast to any changing business priority. Your and your team's job is enabling or contributing to the company's bottom-line, and part of this job is to address the needs of this high-value customer. In such a situation where an urgent requirement is coming from a high-pressure customer and several things including sales, business opportunities are at stake, your only plan is to respond to this business priority fast, and there is no better plan than that. In your new manager's role, if you do not respond to this changing business priorities fast enough, you may risk affecting the jobs of your team members, not to mention other impacts to the business. These team members, by the way, may continue to disagree with whatever 'plan' you make, or your positions, quite the way you would have reacted when you were the trainer yourself.

The same analogy of role and expectations apply to whether you are moving from a learning specialist to a learning manager or from an instructional designer to an instructional design manager.

Remember, in training or learning management role, you will be spending much time watching, monitoring, analyzing and responding to changing business priorities which could only by training related solution.

Therefore, start making this second most important change in your thought process which is to learn how to respond to changing business priorities quickly. Your leadership abilities will become evident based on how effectively you manage this change in you and your team.

CHANGE #3: MANAGEMENT STRATEGIES - STRIKING ALIGNMENT WITH COMPANY AND MANAGEMENT STRATEGIES

Let's see how you may have viewed management approaches and strategies as a trainer, instructional designer or L&D professional:

Recall an occasion when you have seen your training manager driving some new processes which were supposedly claimed to improve the quality of the output. However, you were very skeptical because you feel it may increase the workload instead. There could have times when you rather felt that you probably had some better approaches compared to your manager.

Here is the better part of the truth that someone up higher in the ladder could have introduced those strategies. Top-down hierarchy does play a role in organizational structure.

Let's flip this around and let's see what happens the moment you move up in the management role:

Now, you will be in continuous dialogs with all your stakeholders in regard to what is working and what is not. There will be a continuous scanning of the internal and external environmental factors which was not your job function when you were a trainer. In training management role, these dialogs usually result in framing certain organization level strategies designed to stay efficient, effective and competitive.

The way you never agreed to certain changes as a trainer, you may not even agree now to certain process improvements as a training manager. However, to ensure the highest level of efficiency, your job is to strike the highest level of alignment with organizational strategies. As a member of the management team, you need to speak the same language as your manager, or your chief executive. If you don't, your organization and your role may become short-lived in the cutting edge competition.

Remember, the moment you step up in training and learning management role, you need to understand your organization's competitive strategies, market planning, and long-term business goals and how the proposed process changes will help achieve those goals.

Therefore, the third most important change in the thought process you need to make is to strike the highest level of alignment with organizational strategies. This includes management strategies, market strategies, and your own manager's strategies.

TAKE AWAY

If you are an individual contributor, trainer, instructional designer or a learning professional and planning to move up to training or learning management role, you better start practicing these three changes in your thought process.

a) Finding solutions to customer needs:

Ensure partnership with customers to find a variety of solutions to meet customer needs. Observe and ask your training manager what type of analysis or assessment he is doing to address customer needs.

b) Responding to changing business priorities:

Look beyond the narrow job scope and start responding fast to changing business priorities. Observe how your training manager does it every time he asks you to change your plans. Look what background work he may have done to respond to a given business priority quickly. Try to understand what could be the after effect of not responding or reacting to it.

c) Aligning to the management strategies:

Strike the highest level of alignment with your organizational and market strategies. Read the corporate blog and listen to your chief officers and their thoughts. Ask your manager to share company strategy or reason behind certain changes and how it will help you or your team members to move toward organizational goals.

◆ ◆ ◆ ◆ ◆

Chapter 3

DECISION-MAKING

LEARN 3 CORE SKILLS TO MAKE EFFECTIVE DECISIONS IN TRAINING WORLD

"Decision-making" is the second strategic competency in S2Pro© model of strategic competencies for training and learning management function for developing new training and learning managers. While decision-making is a generic and most fundamental skill in any management function, it requires some additional considerations in training and learning management. S2Pro© model of strategic competencies proposes three core skills to accelerate competency of new training/learning managers in decision-making.

Ability to make decisions is a core management and leadership skill in any domain. In the training arena, this skill could be a savior. Occasionally an individual contributor stepping up from a trainer or learning specialist's role to a management role tend to carry the impression that training and learning manager's role probably required a similar level of skills as needed by any other management role. However, the traditional management training you may have got during your project management course may not help you completely when you take up a training management role. In this chapter, three very critical skills are shared that you may need in your new role in training and learning management.

SKILL #1: PERFORM COMPREHENSIVE STAKEHOLDER ANALYSIS

First of all, you need to ask yourself: Do you know all your stakeholders? Do you know your team of trainers, instructional designers or L&D professionals may also be important stakeholders? Have you considered the impacts of your deliverables and how your important stakeholders would see those impacts?

One of the unique things which separate the training role from any other management role is a mix of stakeholders. Stakeholder analysis is not as simple as it may look like in other management streams. Stakeholders may include account manager, customer manager, marketing managers, operations managers, service manager, finance people, engineering and technical groups to name a few.

Once you have a listed all your stakeholders, then briefly summarize what is that they want from you or your team. It may be a very small but a specific piece of the deliverable. Create a stakeholder matrix out of this information in the form of a table. You might want to list the expectations and deliverables of your stakeholders.

SKILL #2: IMPLEMENT CLEAR STAKEHOLDER COMMUNICATION

Do you have the plan how you keep all stakeholders on the same page? Have you updated all your stakeholders regarding a decision? Have you included and aligned well with all your stakeholders? And last but not least, what type of communication style is required to work effectively with various stakeholders?

Let me caution you that, your new stakeholders will not speak your training language. Most of your stakeholders will be speaking a non-training language different from your language if you are a seasoned training professional. While the executives understand the language of 'business performance' and not of training per se, your customers will speak the language of 'workforce capabilities,' and most probably your field folks might be using the language of numbers and money.

You need to be able to talk your stakeholder language and need to have clear communication in their language. Does it require you to above and beyond your job role? Probably yes, at times. Nevertheless, it would pay off in the long run.

SKILL #3: DEVELOP SOUND STRATEGY FOR STAKEHOLDER EXPECTATIONS MANAGEMENT

Do you have a strategy to manage the expectations of all your stakeholders? Do you know reasonable and unreasonable expectations of your stakeholders? Have you clarified the expectations? Do you know who is merely a participant in the discussion and who the decision-maker is?

The complexity of stakeholders' management in the training domain may not become evident instantly to you, but eventually, this becomes a key capability you may need to become a successful training manager. The reason why stakeholder management in the training role is a little more sophisticated than other management role is the complexity of decisions in the training area and several different angles involved at various layers of stakeholder interface.

Are the decisions made in a training domain really that complex? Some, yes. At first, several budding training managers do not realize the complexity of training related decisions. The decision-making in the training domain is not simple, although it might look simple at the surface. If the training department is a core element of the support system in an organization, any decision made related to training is likely to lead to several chain reactions across the entire support system. A simple decision in training operations may have multi-fold such as customer satisfaction, gaining or losing business, the risk of losing know-how, market positioning as well as other strategies in the company.

Let me elaborate with an example. Suppose your new job is to manage training on a product or process which embodies certain know-how, which may be considered as a trade secret by your organization. What would you do if your key customer asks you to deliver an advanced training program that may put your years of a regimented policy of safeguarding your trade secret at risk? You may be at a delicate line of where it may be hard to decide between losing strategic know-how versus losing the business form the customer. Naturally, you start approaching your stakeholders to make a reasonable decision. Now, look at this situation from other stakeholders' perspective for a moment. The account manager responsible for revenue from the customer is your stakeholder. He may be more concerned about satisfying the customer needs even though some of those may be unreasonable. He might think that his subsequent business dealings with the customer may be adversely affected depending on how well you address a customer's current request. Similarly, the marketing folks, another stakeholder for you, may see it an opportunity to 'sell' a new solution or to make revenue from this request. The design folks, one of your stakeholders, may think it as a request that may put the competitiveness of the organization on the line. That's how decision-making in such complex stakeholder environment becomes high-stake depending upon which angle you adopt.

As a new training manager, you most likely will be focused on what skills customer is interested in and how you are going to give that solution to him. Take a moment and ponder over this disconnect you may face concerning the other business stakeholders. You may have conflicting opinions.

TAKE AWAY

In your new role of training or learning management, you need to extremely conscious about this stakeholder portfolio, and you need to connect to business needs and business strategies to be successful.

When you transition to a training management role, one of the key responsibilities you will have is to convert uncertainty into certainty. You need to run your training operations, projects, programs, and team activities with a very high degree of reliability.

As a training leader, to bring this reliability and clarity, you need to manage stakeholder analysis, stakeholder communication and overall management of stakeholder expectations in light of the business needs.

◆ ◆ ◆ ◆ ◆

Chapter 4

OPERATIONS

MANAGEMENT

MASTER 3 PILLARS OF RELIABLE TRAINING OPERATIONS MANAGEMENT

"Operations Management" is the third strategic competency in S2Pro© model of strategic competencies for training and learning management function for developing new training and learning managers. Operations management of training function takes a larger chunk of a manager's time making it a highly important competency. S2Pro© model of strategic competencies proposes three foundational pillars that a new training/learning manager need to master to accelerate his/her operations management competency.

Generally speaking, a typical training or learning manager spends most of their time in managing operations. The training operations management, in nature and goal, is no different from operations management in any other domain. It takes a few foundational best practices to excel in operations management.

When you transition to a training management role, one of the key responsibilities you will have is to convert uncertainty into certainty. You need to run your training operations, projects, programs, and team activities with a very high degree of reliability. In general, any operational aspect of the business including training operations would have following KPIs:

- **Efficiency** (how fast your training operations respond to customer needs),
- **Effectiveness** (how well you meet customer needs) and
- **Quality** (how robust your deliverable are).

How are you going to achieve these KPIs? In this chapter, I share three most important ingredients/elements of infrastructure you would need to manage well to manage overall training operations effectively. Having a great handle on these three elements right from the beginning will make you a successful training or learning manager whose operations management can deliver reproducible and repeatable results with reliability.

These three elements of an effective and reliable operations management are:

a) **Processes**

b) **Systems**

c) **Structure**

Let's talk about each one of them one-by-one:

PILLAR #1: PROCESSES - THE "HEART" OF THE TRAINING ORGANIZATION

Processes are the HEART of the training and learning operations. The processes are fundamental building blocks of any successful training and learning organization. Any training or learning department spans across a range of processes, no matter the scale of operations. Any activity can be converted into the process if it is required to be performed several times and there are chances of large variability when several different people are running the same activity. When an activity is made as a process, it usually becomes man-independent activity. The processes range from enrollments, scheduling, train-the-trainer, training request from customers, participant orientations, processes inside the classroom, processes for evaluation etc. to name a few.

In simple words, the process is an arrangement that ensures that it produces a predictable, reliable and repeatable outcome every time for a given set of inputs.

For longer-term reliability, actions performed to improve training operations cannot be as simple as tracking of "open/close" status of action items (as is usually done in the project management context). Rather, the actions require additional thought process for permanent fixes. Such an expectation of a high level of reliability from training operations to be more reliable, processes plays a great role in building a culture which emphasizes finding 'permanent fixes' whenever any operational issue is detected.

The output of one process may be fed into another process. Thus robustness of each of the process is very crucial for failure-proof operations. A focus on processes is very important ingredients of successful training operations.

How would you acquire this?

Well, this has a lot to do with your process orientation. Process mapping is one powerful skill which requires thinking and tools to represent the workflow of any operation or process. Why is process mapping important? This will help you clarify inputs, outputs, and failure-points of a process. This also helps you present your case for improvements to your team and your manager.

Some tips that may help you to strengthen this pillar in your new role are as follows:-

– Develop a high-level process map for the department operations under you. To begin with, just represent the component processes as blocks. That will help you gauge the quantum and range of processes you and your team may be employing.

– Given the amount of the processes you may have, it may not always be feasible to map out all of them in one go. Take it slow. Focus on the most crucial processes first, which may impact the company bottom-line results if executed with errors. Map those first.

– Delegate your team members to draft the process map or service blueprint of the processes they use very often with a focus on inputs and outputs. Such sub-process can be integrated slowly over-time with the high-level process allowing you to create a department level blueprint.

Process orientation is an extremely valuable skill in learning and training domain. Training and learning are continuous processes, and thus a process orientation is rather the most basic skill expected from training management professional.

PILLAR #2: SYSTEMS - THE "MIND" OF THE TRAINING ORGANIZATION

Systems in any organizations act as the MIND of the organization. Systems are interconnected components or elements which work together to transform a set of inputs into the desired output. A systems view allows understanding how an organization or a BU is operating. Some examples of the systems you may have are LMS system, customer management tracking system, etc.

Training and learning processes are typically designed around several such interconnected systems. Usually, systems and processes go hand-to-hand. Your training operations may have a system of how customer training demand is captured or logged. And you may have a process how you decide on entertaining those requests.

Processes usually define what we are going to do with the information and how it will be processed. As the business or operations evolve or change, the processes are subject to improvement and change at the same time. But the systems within which these processes operate are expected to be stable.

In several instances, systems and processes may mean the same thing. Again, it also depends on what you view as a system and what you view as components of the system. On one side you may consider your enrollment management system as a system which consists of several processes like how someone will make a training request, how the training requests will be responded to, how the pricing of training will be computed to name a few. On the other side, you may call training request logging "process" as a system if this acts independently of others and if you are simply using it to take the requests and process in some other system.

Nevertheless, you need to know that systems are the memory infrastructure for the organization and these are supposed to be stable and act as load-bearing pillars.

How would you ensure that your systems are stable?

Over the years of experience in the training area, I observed that managers possessing systems approach to operations are far more successful than the managers who rely only on process orientation. A systems approach is a disposition whereby you develop an ability to view a larger organization composed of its elements and interconnection among those components.

The processes you defined earlier would help you. Now need to start thinking the connection of various processes within a system or among several systems. Develop a knack for system thinking. This will help you assess how information flows in and out of the systems and will also help you assess the efficiency, effectiveness, and quality of the training operations.

PILLAR #3: STRUCTURE - THE "BODY" OF THE TRAINING ORGANIZATION

Structure plays a great role in putting systems and processes together into a fully functional unit. This acts as the body of the training organization. The structure provides clarity to the training operations. Very often you will encounter this question from your internal or external customer that "how are your solutions structured?" or "how is your training operations structured?"

In reality, the structure may be all pervasive ranging from your team members, to your meetings, to your e-mail communication to your customer training offerings. When you group your team members by project, you create a structure. When you assign one person for a certain type of communication and interactions, you create the structure.

How would you ensure that your structure is efficient?

When you change the structure within a system or among several systems, it may have a profound impact on the overall training efficiency and effectiveness. Processes and systems certainly help you maintain reliable operations, but structure plays an important role in operational efficiency. Processes and systems are basically carriers which help structure stay stable.

Thus, the 'body' of the training operations is a structure which makes the operations visible and tangible to the external and internal customers. As a general rule by structuring the systems correctly, you can get rid of several redundant processes and overall operations will become reliable and repeatable. This will help you achieve efficiency, effectiveness, and quality in training activities.

TAKE AWAY

As a training manager, one of the crucial responsibilities you will have to design and develop a viable structure of how your systems are connected or arranged in doing your training operations and projects. Your goal will be to employ an efficient structure (or structures) which result in stable systems and effective hassle-free processes.

Further readings

Note that literature may present different definition of processes, systems, and structure from several different perspectives.

Further reading is available here: *Systems, Processes, and Structures* at http://www.researchgate.net/publication/2501724_Systems_Proce sses_and_Structures/file/79e4150ed692d4cbfb.pdf.

A useful resource to know more about systems vs. processes is *Systems and Processes- Is there any differences?* At http://www.thecqi.org/Documents/community/South%20Western/W essex%20Branch/Systems%20and%20Processes%20article%20by%20 David%20Hoyle%20Oct09%20(2).pdf.

A useful reference to read about the relationship between systems and structure is here: *Systems and Structure* at http://www.marxists.org/reference/archive/spirkin/works/dialecti cal-materialism/ch02-s07.html.

♦ ♦ ♦ ♦ ♦

Chapter 5

TRAINING MANAGEMENT

ADOPT 3 HIGHLY SUCCESSFUL TRAINING MANAGEMENT PRACTICES

"Training Management" is the fourth strategic competency in S2Pro© model of strategic competencies for training and learning management function for developing new training and learning managers. Training management requires additional competencies over and above any other standard management role. S2Pro© model of strategic competencies proposes three core practices to accelerate training management competency of new training/learning managers.

If you have been managing operations and projects in learning and training function, then you may have made some unique observation.

Training and learning management requires successful management of "operations" and "projects" at the same time. Yes, the coexistence of the activities under these two characteristically different domains with equal intensity at the same time has been making training and learning function a unique one.

I came across a very interesting definition of Operation and Projects which states the organization, operations and projects is one big happy family [from http://anishmathaimathew.wordpress.com]:

- *The organization is the parent*
- *Operations is the responsible elder brother*
- *The project is the flamboyant younger brother*

During my research, I found that successful training organizations leverage this unique overlay of operations management and project management. They are seen managing operations efficiently and projects effectively. Such organizations have been driving radical improvement in their business outcomes much faster than their competitors through the highly synergetic overlay of efficient operations and effective projects to meet customer needs. Their success relative to their competitors depends on how well they drive synergy between these two functions.

This coexistence of operation management and project management activities is all pervasive in several other business functions as well these days. However, in training and learning management function, it is extremely important to harness the power of these two functions to achieve overall business success.

We also found that these leading organizations made it a point to instill powerful operations and project management skills in their training and learning managers. Most successful learning leaders have been seen to possess these two skills (operations management and project management) at the same time and leverage these skills with dexterity to drive business improvements.

This chapter elaborates on how these two domains are strategically interrelated. As a new training and learning manager, you need to adopt the following 3 practices in your work style.

PRACTICE #1: MANAGING OPERATIONS EFFICIENTLY

Operations are the ongoing, routine activities that are involved in the organization's primary business. This is the "keeping-the-lights-on" work, such as staffing management, payroll, product production, service delivery, etc. As such, operations include all of the "normal" business functions.

Some of the examples of operations are: day-to-day job of offering courses, managing resources, securing trainers, assigning tasks to instructional designers, responding to customer inquiries, seeking feedback, handling escalations, providing guidance and managing team, attending meetings and requests from business units, checking financial and budgetary standing, making strategic plans, managing facility and equipments among several others.

After talking to training and learning managers from several different industries, we found that, for most of them, their operations spanned across several business units, stakeholders, departments, contributors and activities. Wide range of KPIs are typically associated with each operation. This makes the training and learning job highly dynamic and never boring for them!!!

The real business success of a training organization is not measured by how well it can execute the projects (which are one-time-off efforts) but by its operations in terms of:

- How well can it run operations flawlessly to support internal and external customers?
- How fast can it respond to customer needs?
- How quickly can it accommodate changing business situations?
- How reliable and dependable its operations are?
- How robust is it in the time of catastrophe?

This is just a glimpse of several different indicators that shows the health of the training organization.

In our research, most of the training and managers indicated that they spend 75% of their days' time handling and managing operations!!!

Isn't it amazing?

Some managers said they enjoy the dynamism in the operations and for others, it was a mundane job with nothing new. The latter categories of the managers were from a project management mindset who enjoy time-driven and time-bound challenges, as opposed to ongoing activities.

The size and industry of the organization could make the operations even complex, random, and unpredictable. Such randomness in operations is also driven by the need for a faster response to situations, customer needs, and business priorities. The organization's management itself sometimes underrates skills required to manage and handle operations. However, skills to manage operations are crucial to the success of the organization since the overall efficiency of training function depends on how operations are being conducted. The intertwined operations require training and learning managers to be extremely good at multitasking, the superb priority management, great in time management and most importantly the ability to filter the noise vs. signal.

Therefore a higher level of skills (much higher than project management) are required to run successful operations. A certain level of breadth in skills is crucial for being successful in handling training and learning operations.

PRACTICE #2: MANAGING PROJECTS EFFECTIVELY

According to PMI's *PMBOK® Guide* (2008), a project is "a temporary endeavor undertaken to create a unique product, service, or result." Thus, a project is temporary in nature, having a defined start and end date, and produces a unique output. Projects are conducted as a means to obtain the organization's strategic objectives above and beyond normal organizational operations.

Examples of projects may be facility consolidation, use of new technology, specific gap analysis, stop-gap arrangement, customized solution design, new implementations, cost reduction of operation and specific course development among several others.

Projects are the adrenaline of the organizations which keep them thrusting forward to drive major improvements. The organizations highly focused on customer and improvement usually drive several projects. Research shows that an established organization fundamentally implement a new operation first testing as a project. Highly successful projects result in the implementation of long-term stable operations.

Several training managers enjoy this aspect of the job because it provides them with new challenges which change in nature as they move to the next project. These time-driven and time-bound activities keep their interest level up and high. In most cases, such managers are seen to have come from the non-training background. Generally, the training managers exhibiting the traditional mindset that a project is a one-time-off event, usually find it hard to relate to or stay interested in managing operations efficiently.

Our research showed that training and learning managers spend about 25% of their time in driving projects. It is much lower than the time they have been spending on the operations.

Skills required to effectively managing the projects are universally known. Now, does the training domain require a different kind of project management skills? Not, really. However, the project management in training and learning domain is indeed slightly more complex because learning is a continuous phenomenon.

The projects in the learning domain are more of continuous efforts than a one-time event. This characteristic of "continuity" basically makes nature of projects in the training domain very similar to operations. Thus, basic operations management skills come handy while the projects in training and learning domain.

PRACTICE #3: SYNERGIZING PROJECTS AND OPERATIONS

It has been seen that just strong project management skills are not enough for being a successful training and learning leader. Then what do you need to become a successful training and learning leader? It is: *managing both operations and projects efficiently and effectively.*

PMBOK (2008) points out that both projects and operations have processes like planning, executing, controlling stages and also people perform both of them and constrained by limited resources. So if these two concepts have a considerable amount of similarities, then what makes a project differ from an operation? Let's talk about success in operations vs. projects. How it differs?

Operations are ongoing and intended to sustain the business. They do not have any end date. As said before, projects are conducted to attain an objective and then terminate, organize activities that are not supported under the organization's normal operations and are directly related to the achievement of the organization's strategic plan. Thus, it is very important to be conscious about time allocation on the both. Our research indicates that training managers typically spend 75% of their time on operations management and 25% on the project management. Since projects are time-bound, training managers may need a higher level of energy and focus on producing results aggressively.

OPERATIONS

FROZEN STABLE PATTERN

- Functional organization
- Line management
- Ongoing
- Day-to-day activities
- Functional and operational processes
- Standing roles and Responsibilities
- Protect continuity
- Resource constraints
- Single loop: efficiency

PROJECTS

UNFREEZE – CHANGE –REFREEZE

- Project organization
- Project management
- Project activities
- Temporary
- Project scope
- Time constraints
- Project management processes
- Project roles and responsibilities
- Double loop: effectiveness

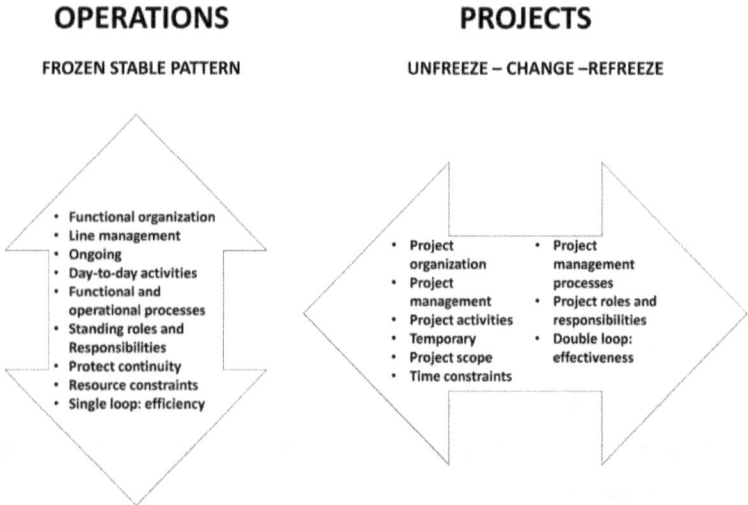

Operations versus Projects (Image is courtesy SAP-Press)

Operational priorities may sometimes override project priorities. Both operation management and project management require solid priority management and time management skills.

In operations management, you are being measured for efficiency while in the project you are being measured across several dimensions which includes quality, cost, schedule- in short effectiveness.

For project management, you are accountable for a certain part of the project or the full project itself and therefore, you have stakes in the failure and success of the same. For managing operations, you are fully responsible for the failure or success of the operations, most of the time, as a single owner.

These are two different worlds.

Research shows that managers, who are capable of converting project outcomes into long-term continuous operational improvements and set milestones for them, are highly successful in both the worlds of operations and projects. They are not only strong project leaders but also strong training operations managers too.

TAKE AWAY

Now you are stepping into a role which requires you to be best in both the world; you might want to take note of two tips to become a successful training and learning leader.

1. **Run your operations by converting it into processes to the extent possible.** By mapping operations in the form of processes, you can save your energy, reduce your firefighting and improve overall efficiency. Refer to Part III of this e-book on using processes, structures, and systems to streamline operations.

2. **Convert the outcomes of your project into long-term tiered or continuous operational improvement milestones.** Never lose the focus on how project outcomes can be transformed into standard operations or processes. Refer to the next chapter on long-term continuous improvements while managing projects.

♦ ♦ ♦ ♦ ♦

Chapter 6

PROJECT LEADERSHIP

CHOOSE 2 POWERFUL STYLES TO LEAD LEARNING & TRAINING PROJECTS

"Project Leadership" is the fifth strategic competency in S2Pro© model of strategic competencies for training and learning management function for developing new training and learning managers. While project management is a singular specialized skill in other streams, in training domain project management requires characteristically different orientation focusing on long-term outcomes and process improvement. S2Pro© model of strategic competencies proposes two unique styles to accelerate project leadership competency of new training/learning managers in training domain.

What would be your style when you start leading and managing the learning projects?

Let me share with you two different types of management styles you may come across in training and learning area. Suppose you have been assigned a project to improve some key aspect of your employees' learning environment in particular settings. How would you proceed with to manage it?

In my research, two different styles emerged which are quite commonly adopted by training and learning managers:

STYLE #1: PROJECT MANAGEMENT STYLE OF LEADING LEARNING PROJECTS

During my research, I came across training and learning managers whose style was quite project management focused. They displayed a great sense of action and mostly took most of the learning activities as one-time action with the focus on closing the actions which could give immediate visible results. That's what the first style of project leadership all about.

With this style of management, you exhibit a very action focused outlook. You will charge on to the project, start converting it into some achievable and measurable targets. You will also define some key KPIs which become the success criteria for your project. After all, you want to be successful and want to see your efforts becoming successful. Next, you will start building a plan which starts with dates and ends with dates. Your project plan may involve several tasks and activities. You may be tracking each task with actions on it, consciously monitoring the open/close status of each task. Your task-focus will help you close all outstanding actions well on time with minimal impact on the project schedule, resources, cost and quality. That's great project management leadership. Yes, you can drive the project to a meaningful closure and be a successful training project manager.

The philosophy has an analogy – "Grow the crop and harvest it". That means you put efforts in growing the crops in every season, and then you harvest it in every season. Next time, you start with zero again and go through the cycle again (next project). The philosophy that drives such a style is that improvements targeted as part of the KPIs are one-time targets. This philosophical outlook leads you to handle the project that way – one-time deal.

Most organizations advocate the project management style of this kind because they train their managers with standard project management methodology. As such this project leadership style is well-established, equipped with millions of tips all around the internet and lot of tools to maintain that focus.

When this project is closed, is it truly over for you as a training manager? Yes, if you have been handling it as a project manager mindset. No, not yet, if you were true training or learning manager. In our research, it showed that when such a philosophy is adopted, several training/learning managers found themselves in a trap of re-instituting similar project with similar or same KPIs a couple of years later again. So work was not truly driven to closure.

STYLE #2: PROCESS MANAGEMENT STYLE OF LEADING LEARNING PROJECTS

I came across several highly successful learning leaders who go beyond the borders of focusing on immediate open/close action on the tasks as is usually done in any standard project management. They leaped several steps ahead of project boundaries to produced repeatable, recurring, continuous results. They were exhibiting second style of project leadership.

With this style of management, you will still be displaying the same level of great project leadership as explained in the previous style. The one limitation is that it is time-bound. So your targeted KPIs must hit the target by the end date.

However, there is another style of project leadership in training domain in which you will take a different approach which is much larger in scope and spectrum compared to your original project scope. Here your KPIs won't be any different from what it was before. However, as a training/learning managers, you would extend project KPIs into different bands or phases and will implement remaining KPIs through operational improvements. For example, if your project KPIs were to achieve an X level of quality, then you would extend these KPIs to Y, Z over the years with measurable improvements in operational aspects and processes that surrounds the activity under question. Your job as a training manager would not end until you achieve those tiered KPIs beyond the scope of your original project.

The point is that for you, targets will not be stationary unlike that of a scoped time-bound project. For you even if the project is officially over, still you will continuously keep monitoring it and very occasionally keep raising the bars of improvement targets to next quality level. You will continuously evaluate the results and effectiveness of your project's outcomes in the context of improvement in the overall operations and processes. You will continuously make adjustments in the associated operations surrounding the activities under the project scope. You will keep setting/raising KPIs for the operations in tiered fashion which may not be part of the time-bound project scope.

The analogy here is "Grow the tree and reap the fruits every season". That means you invest your time in growing and nurturing a tree for long-term fruits you get every season. If you are managing learning projects this way, you will be a manager who does not just focus on short-term gains and immediate results; rather you stay focused on long-term gains and continuous results that come with a parallel focus on operations. This continuous focus on quality and effectiveness is a crucial success to your success in leading training and learning projects.

Doing so sets your project leadership style apart when leading learning and training management function. Your continuous focus will drive much more value-addition to the business over and above what the first approach would have added.

TAKE AWAY

While the first style is reaping crop once and harvest it, the latter style is like reaping trees which gives fruits every season. Now, why so much emphasis on later style? Because learning is a continuous process, and it does not stop anywhere. Learning transformation and learning improvements are not achieved instantly. It sometimes takes years to notice the impact of certain project implementations. Therefore learning projects requires a key component of process management and continuous improvement tied closely with moving tiered targets rather than the stationary ones, of course, every time the targets keep moving upwards.

So when you take a leadership role in managing learning and training function, what type of management philosophy you would take leading your projects?

♦ ♦ ♦ ♦ ♦

Chapter 7

STRATEGIC LEADERSHIP

FOLLOW 10 STRATEGIC APPROACHES TO STANDOUT AS GREAT LEARNING MANAGEMENT LEADER

"Strategic Leadership" is the sixth strategic competency in S2Pro© model of strategic competencies for training and learning management function for developing new training and learning managers. Strategic thinking and strategic leadership are no longer only an upper management function, rather it is a front-line requirement. Training leaders require some characteristically different approaches to establish their strategic leadership. S2Pro© model of strategic competencies reveals ten approaches to accelerate strategic leadership competency of new training/learning managers.

Are you a business-as-usual training or learning manager? Do you aspire to be a training management leader? Have you ever wondered what sets the leading and well-known training management leaders apart from business-as-usual training management? I pondered upon several questions like following.

- What differentiates them from common training managers or learning management professionals?
- How they show leadership in managing large-scale complex training operations?
- How they drive and thrive projects?
- How they view learning design?
- How they lead teams and organizations?
- How they plan, strategize and execute missions?
- How do they transform from simple training professionals to thought leaders?
- What makes them the thought leaders?

During our research through extended research by conducting surveys and systematic analysis of profiles, resumes and career paths of several hundreds of leading training management leaders, we found that several common patterns emerged. They were seen to adopt 10 key approaches not usually seen in business-as-usual training managers.

Here are those 10 approaches we think new training/learning managers should follow to accelerate their long-term development.

APPROACH #1. STAY CURRENT ON THE NEXT-GEN RESEARCH AND PRACTICES IN LEARNING VS. USING TIME-TESTED PROVEN METHODS

Studies show that highly successful training leaders tend to use 'hot-from-oven' methodologies and techniques without having to wait for it to get adopted by others. Successful training leaders usually advocate such early research models which become industry adoption sooner or later.

Looking at training leaders' resumes and profiles, we find that they are actively participating in years' engagement with leading professional forums and engaged in research and practice in the area of training. Some of them have also shown an extended association with the academic world like universities or even journals too. It would not be uncommon for you to see training leaders possessing a higher research degree or even a doctorate.

You may want to adopt this must-have trait of the successful training leaders. As a training management leader, you would not just depend on time-tested best practices alone. Rather, you will challenge the equations. If you are keen on developing yourself as a training management leader, why not associate yourself to some form of research?

The bottom-line is that research in any form (can be just practice-oriented, survey-based or simply interviews) is a key success contributor to shape you as a training management leader. Such an engagement enables training management leaders to bring new practices, BKMs and techniques to their work to gain a competitive edge in the marketplace.

You may read some details in Chapter 9 on professional development on expanding your portfolio.

APPROACH #2. THINK ABOUT TOTAL LEARNING EXPERIENCE DESIGN VS. JUST THE INSTRUCTIONAL DESIGN

This key mindset differentiates the training management leaders from business-as-usual training management professionals. Studies show that training leaders tend to look at overall learning experience design as opposed to instructional design only. Let me clarify how these two differs.

Total learning experience design focuses not just at what needs to be done to design a course (which is the field of instructional design), but it mainly focuses on the whole spectrum of activities. These activities span over designing the learning environment, learning media, training infrastructure, learning enablement processes, learning transfer, post-training learning, use of performance support tools, monitoring of performance at the job and finally the linkage of learning with the business result. This learning experience design also includes informal learning which is pretty much excluded in standard instructional design.

While the instructional design is necessary for training organizations, the learning leaders are seen focusing on end-to-end learning 'experience' design. If you are keen on developing yourself as a training management leader, why not start expanding your horizon of activities beyond instructional design?

APPROACH #3. ALWAYS IN SYNC WITH THE BUSINESS NEEDS VS. JUST THE TRAINING NEEDS

Studies show that training management leaders focus on customer or business needs as opposed to training needs. Although training may be viewed as an important mechanism to solve several organizational performance problems, however, training may not be the only solution for a given business situation.

To become a training management leader, you need to expand focus away from thinking that training is the only solution in a given business situation. If you are an instructional designer, you may need to understand that designing a course may not always be the first solution. A larger percentage of your analysis, planning for a solution and recommendations may be concentrated on the business needs and may not even convert into a real training session.

You may want to read Chapter 2 of this book regarding the importance of aligning well with business needs.

APPROACH #4. USE PROCESS SKILLS MORE OFTEN THAN PROJECT MANAGEMENT SKILLS

Studies show that training management leaders are more focused on processes rather than just projects. Training management leaders do not just focus on short-term gains and immediate results; rather they stay focused on long-term gains and continuous results. This continuous focus on quality and effectiveness is a crucial trait to be successful in leading training and learning projects.

If you want to be a training management leader, you will need to take a different approach to the projects which may include KPIs tied to operations, tiered or phased success criteria on operational improvements.

You can read more about this in Chapter 6 of this book on 2 powerful styles to lead learning projects.

APPROACH #5. PLAN FOR AN EXTENDED HORIZON VS. JUST SHORT-TERM CLOSURE OF ACTION ITEMS

Training and learning environment is unique in the sense that actions performed in this environment are usually not a simple one-off "open/close" status of several actions. Rather it requires permanent fixes. To ensure results are reproducible, training management leaders are seen to build a culture of 'permanent fix' into their training operations.

The leading training management leaders have understood a basic philosophy very well that *learning is a continuous process, and it does not stop anywhere.* Thus, learning transformation and learning improvements are not achieved instantly. It sometimes takes years to notice the impact of certain project implementations.

If you want to be a training management leader, you need to look at the extended horizon of operations. For you, targets will not be stationary and not just one-time off. Rather it is a form of tiered targets or tiered success criteria spanned over several operations over extended periods of time. For you even if an action item is closed for now, still you will continuously keep monitoring it, and very occasionally you will keep raising the bars of improvement targets to next quality level. You can read more about this in Chapter 6 of this book on 2 powerful styles to lead learning projects.

APPROACH #6. STAY FOCUSED ON INTEGRATING TRAINING, LEARNING AND KNOWLEDGE MANAGEMENT

The studies showed that the training managing leaders do not see training as a separate function within a company, rather they view training business unit as an integrating unit which connects the organizational learning and organizational knowledge as two interdependent functions.

In several organizations, while there are several avenues of knowledge generation and capture, they use the training department as the only source of channeling the correct knowledge to the correct audience. Studies revealed that training leaders continuously keep questioning how different business units inside the company are producing knowledge, how the knowledge so produced is being processed and how this processed knowledge is being made available to the audience though training department. Training management leaders value this channelized knowledge as the essential ingredient of continuous learning at the actual workplace.

To become a training management leader and to set yourself apart from business-as-usual training managers, you need to pay attention to organizational knowledge management infrastructure to develop and deliver robust organizational learning. This actually might mean stretching yourself out from training comfort zone and venturing into the knowledge management domain to gain holistic exposure.

APPROACH #7. CONSIDER TRAINING AS A COSTLY BUT ESSENTIAL INVESTMENT

Yes, that's how leaders in training view a training program. Studies show that training management leaders view training as an investment in people, processes, and resources to gain a business advantage. There is an interesting aspect to this postulation- if training management leaders consider training as an investment, does it means that the return on investment (ROI) must be their number one agenda too? Studies showed that this postulation is not always correct. Training management leaders have been seen not to be very fussy about calculating ROI. The analysis shows that training management leaders use quite a bit of intuition and common-sense as opposed to the sophisticated calculation of the ROI of training. They have been mostly seen talking about the cost of mistakes or cost of non-training or cost of non-proficiency, and metrics like that as opposed to the monetary benefits of the training program to the company. They focus on eliminating the waste, errors, mistakes and poor results as opposed to showing fancy numbers in ROI.

Well, it is tough to acquire the visionary intuition. However, staying grounded in the fundamental premise of the training is a starting point. If you can show the financial cost of additional hours spent by an employee due to the absence of training, ROI comes intuitively to the executive staff. You don't have to compute it for them.

APPROACH #8. ALWAYS STAY INFRASTRUCTURE SAVVY

Our research showed that training management leaders are extremely up-to-date with the infrastructure which supports training, learning and knowledge processes. For them, it is the backbone of survival and staying competitive. It has been seen that they know the impact of delay in passing the correct training or information or skill to the employees. The training management leaders demonstrate an understanding that the correct media, correct platform and correct mechanism need to be deployed appropriately to achieve effectiveness in training.

Whether it is LMS, video streaming platform, e-learning, documentation delivery platform, workforce skill tracking or otherwise, they have the global view of the transactions happening at various layers and among various stakeholders to effectively impart the desired learning experience to the employees. That's why most of the training management leaders are seen experimenting with new channels like mobile learning, just-in-time delivery, video-based learning, social media and several other platforms enabling training and learning and constantly in a zest to bring the best technology to equip training.

The competitive value of strategic training is enhanced by the latest technologies, infrastructure and associated processes. Keeping pace with technology and infrastructure is critical for next-generation learning where most of the learning is happening in the workplace setting beyond the boundaries of the training courses. If you need to bring the new generation revolution, you better get on top of the latest infrastructure and develop technical aptitude to appreciate, use and compare new technologies. Ironically, in several companies infrastructure function usually is handled by different people. So you might have to own a few of those things.

To set yourself apart from traditional training managers, you need to pay due attention to infrastructure and keep looking for transformations you need to drive. There is a general tendency in established training departments that they are usually reluctant to change infrastructure if the current infrastructure is giving nominal results.

APPROACH #9. EXPRESS OPINIONS AND DEVELOP MEDIA PRESENCE

Yes, this was found to one of the interesting differentiators. Although training management professional turns leader in their daily job but establishing themselves as subject matter, and strategy expert globally or within a certain circle does not come so easy. Our analysis showed that leading training management leaders are very active on things like blogs, social media channels and other content generation channels. Several of them are seen to be well-published too. Leading training management leaders usually present at well-known training conferences and their articles/papers are considered being an authority in their area.

Simply get started with your blog, publish your articles, write about your best experience and if possible present at industry relevant conferences. Presenting in select webinars may also be great. If you are a good presenter, then YouTube video channel could provide you with great presence. For writing-focused individuals, there are other tons of social media avenues to leverage.

APPROACH #10. DESIGN ROBUST PERFORMANCE SUPPORT SYSTEM FOR CONTINUOUS LEARNING

I purposely kept this differentiator at the end of this chapter. This has been seen in our research as the most powerful differentiator which determine the extent of business success of the training programs led by these training management leaders.

The training management leaders not only focus on the reform in training function itself, but they pay particular attention on how an employee is going to be supported at the workplace after the training. This includes a kind of job aids, tools, and other processes that will support his performance in real-world environment and how he is going to stay proficient in the skills he is trained upon. The fundamental premise here is to chalk out the path for continuous learning after the training. The training leaders transform the performance support systems in such a way that acquired skills eventually result in long-term behavior change and continuous learning at the workplace. That's how these training management leaders can break away the boundaries of training and become learning leaders.

Next time when you are leading a training program, you need to ask the questions regarding performance support system available to the employee at the workplace when he is out of the training. You need to question how his manager will support him after the training. You need to question the job aids and tools he will be equipped with during his real job. You also need to question how his performance is being measured in real-world settings. You may need to look at the documentation, knowledge, and infrastructure available to employees to perform their job effectively.

♦ ♦ ♦ ♦ ♦

Chapter 8

GLOBAL TEAM

LEADERSHIP

USE 3 PRINCIPLES TO EFFECTIVELY LEAD YOUR NEW DIVERSE GLOBAL TRAINING TEAM

"Global Team Leadership" is the seventh strategic competency in S2Pro© model of strategic competencies for training and learning management function for developing new training and learning managers. While team leadership is a core responsibility of any manager's role, this encompasses more global and cultural challenges. S2Pro© model of strategic competencies suggests three principles to accelerate global team leadership competency of new training/learning managers.

As an individual contributor planning to step up to training management role, you are bound to see plenty of cultural diversity in the globalized training world. Training teams are now composed of trainers, designers, and specialists all across the globe. As a result, they do come with their cultural baggage. Thus, the moment you take up a role in training and learning management, one of the key competencies you would need immediately is to display sufficient level of cultural sensitivity and ability to work with diverse cultural backgrounds within your team. This won't come all of a sudden to you just by a change in your title. You need to start preparing right now.

CHALLENGES IN MANAGING A DIVERSE, MULTI-CULTURAL, GLOBAL TRAINING TEAM

You already may have great experience working with the audience and stakeholders from different countries and cultures. That's great. Still, your new role may offer you new challenges when you are given the responsibility to manage a multi-cultural training and learning team.

Now let's do the reality check. Just recall how well you worked with your manager from a different culture back then when you were a trainer. You probably had your share of a struggle to get better with him. At times you may even have developed a stereotyped image of people of the country or culture to which your manager belonged. You probably had typecast or stereotyped your manager accordingly or may have labeled your manager as culturally insensitive too. Now, you are going to be standing on the other side of the fence very soon, and you are likely to be experiencing some of those to you as well.

When you step up, the first challenge could start with you itself. Your new role may warrant you to strike a great relationship with your new manager who may also be from a different cultural background than yours. Therefore, it is very important for you to understand his work style which may or may not have streaks of his culture. Adding to this challenge is another dimension if you are given a culturally diverse team while you are still coming up with terms with your cross-cultural manager. You will have to understand the impact of the culture of your team members on the work style, communication, and relationship. Your new role may require you to look at this challenge from the performance and productivity stand-point. It is worth investing time in learning these important things. After all, having a great relationship with the team translates into better work life and better performance for you.

Understanding the team members from different cultures by getting to work with them will be a different experience which cannot be documented easily. No amount of training on cultural sensitively may be enough to help you reorient yourself. Three general principles will help you understand your diverse team better, strike a good rapport with them and at the same time display cultural sensitivity in your new role. You may not become good at this overnight, but you will start getting acceptance in the team, eventually. Culture alone is not responsible for your team members' work style and preferences. Mind that corporate culture will also play a great role in shaping how your team members behave at work. Their experiences with previous managers and their past jobs or locations they served earlier may change their expectations which are different from their cultural preferences. So you need to be careful.

Note: As a disclaimer, examples quoted in this article are for the sake of clarifying the ideas and are mostly based on generic information and observations. It may not be universally applicable to the people of the said culture. I suggest you do your research on the culture with which you are interacting.

PRINCIPLE #1: NON-UNIFORM COMMUNICATION STYLE ACROSS CULTURALLY DIVERSE TEAM

In today's business world, such challenges may have changed, and the impact of culture may have got subdued under heavily pressed corporate norms, culture, and global environment. However, certain preferences in communication styles among the employees as a result of years of cultural upbringing cannot ignored. The difference in communication styles across various cultures has a tremendous organizational impact when it comes to the effectiveness of the team members.

For example, Americans team members tend to be very open and forthright in their communication. On the other hand, Japanese team members may prefer an indirect and respectful way of communication, avoiding direct negative responses. Imagine you have both the guys in the same team and they are working on the same project. Different cultural orientation may result in miscommunication or even throw one of the project members feeling isolated. This may result in some conflict due to 'unsaid' assumptions both parties may be making during the process of communication. Take an example of a simple thing as humor. Role of humor varies with culture, and it may affect how the team harmony builds up. Does your team member's culture consider humor a healthy part of everyday work or is humor at work considered silly and fatuous? Handled inappropriately may hamper team communication. You better be conscious about in what settings humor is being used and with whom.

The best way to understand the differences between you and your team is by due diligence – doing your research ahead of time and talking to colleagues or mentors who know better, or who are from the same culture as your team members. If you are part of a LinkedIn group, you can post a question in a discussion forum. Several websites like GlobeSmart may be helpful to you. This website categorizes the cultural observations by country and by activity. Spend some time browsing through the pages. While managing team of diverse cultures, your knowledge about gestures may come very handy. Take for example the simple gesture of a smile. It is not unusual for Americans to exchange smiles with complete strangers. In India, smiling at unknown female employees can be considered risqué. Further, a harmless sign like the thumbs-up has a very negative meaning for Iranians. Make yourself aware of some gestures that may have unique meanings in your team member's culture. Keep in mind that there is no such thing as a universal form of communication. A very common mistake is to expect other people to think the way you do. Recognizing that other people can have perspectives very different from your own is the first step toward developing a good relationship.

Recognize that work habits and work style are strongly impacted by one's belief and value system which generally comes out of the culture of the individual. You may notice that your team members from Thailand and Japan may obey you to a high degree without any debate or challenge. However, in the same team, you may expect your US team member to challenge and debate with you on operational aspects. As regards to greetings, Americans trainers or designers in your training team may tend to address you by first name, irrespective of your job title. They also expect you to do the same. However, a Korean team member may tend to address you as 'sir' once in a while on e-mails or in person.

As a safe strategy, you need to show your genuine interest in their cultural norms and ask questions if you are not sure. The moment you show that you are amazed by their cultures and it intrigues you genuinely, and you are taking an interest to know it more, they will come forward and help you get better at it. I think at the same time we should know that it is possible that your team members are equally concerned about hurting you culturally as you are concerned about hurting them. So make sure you show them who you are. In case you find that your team members have least the idea about different cultural notions of your culture, subtly and slowly educate them too.

A good idea would be to call them for some family events or gathering.

Nevertheless, communication is the only mechanism available to you to drive the alignment of your team to the organizational goals. If you don't use this mechanism effectively, you end up not meeting your work goals. Your challenge in your new role will be to communicate with team members using different communication styles and still keeping the balance and harmony within the team. You would need to establish a correct line of communication and protocols which improves the clarity of communication within the team and with the stakeholders. Remember not to force a uniform communication style to every team member because their communication patterns are individually grown up as a function of their cultural exposure. If you are pushing them to stick on particular communication pattern, style or protocol, that may push some team members into the uncomfortable zone.

PRINCIPLE #2: VERBAL ARTICULATION BY EVERY TEAM MEMBER

The moment you step up in your new role, you will depend heavily on team meetings as a mechanism to bring everyone on the same page. However, your team members from different cultures may tend to view meetings differently.

Now you will have some challenges setting the expectations and meeting protocols right if you have diverse training team, some of which may show a strong reflection of their own culture or the cultured they lived for quite some time. You will notice that certain individuals may prefer to stay quiet during the meetings and hardly participating in discussions. You need to be cautious about the level of agreement when you have culturally diverse training team members in your meeting. Just an example: Your team members coming from western culture may be quite vocal in expressing the concerns and highlighting flaws. However, you Asian team member may be holding his opinion back, and you will have to touch base with him in private. Your team member from India may say yes to your ideas which may mean he heard you, but it may not mean he agrees with you.

Thus, you as a manager will be responsible for making the meeting productive and set the uniform expectations. Also at the same time, you need to be cautious about everyone's participation level in a culturally diverse team.

John W. Adams in *Guide to Living & Working Abroad* shared an example of meeting dynamics in different countries. As per him, in Germany, a meeting is a vehicle for a manager to exchange information. Employees are expected to be well prepared and do not expect to be questioned or challenged. On the other hand, for British and Dutch managers, it could be a forum for debate ideas and come up with a recommendation and an action plan. Every employee at the meeting is expected to contribute. In France, a meeting is for the boss to announce decisions which have been made elsewhere or to solicit specific information. It is not a forum for debate.

In certain cultures, the business talks during the lunch are considered an encroachment on the employee's break time whereas in other cultures lunch could be a platform or excuse to discuss business issues informally. There is a possibility your Japanese team member finds it hard to accommodate with informal and lose atmosphere in the meeting. So you better watch the cues.

Your challenge will be how you shift gears and at the same time drive the team toward common goals in a meeting. The simplest principle we recommend here is to stay focused on your primary objectives during the meeting. A strong focus on objectives may allow everyone to process the information in the same way, thus minimizing any effect of cultural orientation someone may have. Part of this principle, make sure you have your team members articulate inputs, feedback, concerns explicitly and do not make assumptions about silence.

Also, it may be worthwhile for you to know and understand the kind of culture your team members come from and the geographical locations they have served in the past. These factors may have a profound impact on expectations with which team members attend the meeting. In any case, the work priorities may not always let you become a great social networker, and it may not always permit you being very personal and sociable with your team all the time. Your best friend is your keen observation, ask questions during the meeting when you are not sure and listen to the inputs.

PRINCIPLE #3: PERSONAL CONNECTION AND ACCOUNTABILITY-BASED PRODUCTIVE RELATIONSHIPS

Maintaining a good relationship with a culturally diverse team could be one of the most challenging areas and competence to handle this will not come just by a change in title. You need to start observing the team dynamics in your team right now.

The personal connection may do wonder for you in your new role. Your Southeast Asia team member may expect you to talk about their family life, kids and express concerns over the wellbeing of their family and at a time may expect you to provide them reasonable accommodation at the hour of need. They may expect you to have a good understanding of their culture and may even expect your participation in their cultural traditions. On the other hand, an American or Canadian team member may probably prefer informal once in a while beer get-together way from office boundaries. He may expect you to display a personal connection and interestingly expect you to share a lot about you without really getting too personal. You will have to connect with individual team members of diverse cultures in their 1-to-1 with you while you deliver the consensus and unified messages in your team meetings.

Work norms and work practices sometimes get impacted by cultural backgrounds. For example, you may have a German trainer who would probably start and end work punctually at the stated times, and you would not be able to reach him on weekends. You may have some team member from another culture where it is considered okay to be late and okay to be working long hours even on weekends. You will have to define certain norms in this regards and ensure that every member of the team gets his share to overall productivity in his way and with his style.

An accountability-driven management style will be your savior to start with if you end up with culturally complex teams. Such a system allows you to apply some uniform norms and protocols across the team without rigidly adhering to one communication style. For example, the clauses of confidentiality of salary, grades, raises and other manager-employee conversations are interpreted or handled differently in different cultures. As a general observation, whereas your US team members may strictly abide by the clause of confidentiality, the members from other more closely knit cultures may assume it as normal to talk about their grades, salaries as a normal gossip topic. Such situations are tricky ones. You cannot allow any cultural preferences whatsoever on such norms which are either driven by legal requirements, contract terms or anything that may hamper productivity and performance in the team.

Your job is to ensure the accountability of assignments through uniform standards for all (even if you choose to use non-uniform communication styles). You might need to educate your team members separately. As a manager, you would need to see how and what level of flexibility you will provide to individual team members. But your primary goal remains how you ensure consistent work-related behavior and how you drive your diverse team to stick to same work protocol.

◆ ◆ ◆ ◆ ◆

Chapter 9

PROFESSIONAL

DEVELOPMENT

START WITH 5 STRATEGIES TO BUILD A PORTFOLIO AS A TRAINING AND LEARNING SPECIALIST

"Professional Development" is the eighth strategic competency in S2Pro© model of strategic competencies for training and learning management function for developing new training and learning managers. While other professions advocate skill development within the job function, in the training domain one needs to stay on continuous learning, building professional affiliations, and gathering field experience from external resources beyond the organization. S2Pro© model of strategic competencies guides with five strategies to the professional development of new training/learning managers.

If you are planning to step up in training and learning management role, your previous experience as a trainer, instructional designer, learning specialist or HRD professional may not be sufficient enough to give you a strategic and competitive edge while bidding for a management role. You need to strengthen your portfolio. As an individual contributor, you may have opportunities to work on various assignments to lead or to manage at your workplace. However, you would need a stronger profile to demonstrate the leadership in several domains.

STRATEGY #1: EARN A GLOBAL MANAGEMENT CERTIFICATION

Certification is one of the first steps you may want to take to build your portfolio. Earning certification will give one badge on your profile that reflects that you possess needed specialization. Note the difference between 'certificate,' 'certification' and 'certification that gives a certified designation.' You can choose any based on your budget, time you can devote and meet the qualification criteria.

Some of my old blog posts described a range of certification options in training and learning domain, though dated, the general approach is still valid:

- https://managingtraining.wordpress.com/2013/08/09/professiona
  l-training-learning-management-certifications-gaining-an-edge-
  in-your-new-role/,
- https://managingtraining.wordpress.com/2013/08/13/how-to-
  select-the-appropriate-professional-certification-in-training-and-
  learning-management/,
- https://managingtraining.wordpress.com/2013/08/10/certified-
  designations-in-training-management-enhancing-your-profile-
  in-new-role/

STRATEGY #2: ACQUIRE SOLID PROJECT MANAGEMENT SKILLS

Project management in a general context is the most powerful skill training specialists, and instructional designers have to have. Generally, such specialists get plenty of opportunity working on projects independently. Formal training in project management may be helpful, but remember project management is all about situational skills and you may need real experience to develop that situational understanding.

- **General project management:** To build your portfolio, first you need to develop solid project management skills while you are deployed on certain projects (areas may not matter). It may be as small as lead auditing the best practices of your peers. Once you have such an opportunity, apply the standard body of knowledge to set up some plan and milestones and track the outcomes on a regular basis to start building your project management skills.

You may have to work very productively with your manager to bag such opportunities to taste the waters in a controlled environment, especially where stakes may not be high. He may assign you a project ranging from managing an event for the team to a key customer training project.

- **Domain-specific project management:** Next, you should put some extra effort into bagging projects which matching your areas of interest where the results of the projects add to your portfolio, evidence and real case experience. The opportunity may come as a simple form as doing a cost analysis for an internal and external customer. In training and learning domain, several times several allied activities may come in the form of tasks.

You need to keep your ears and eyes open to see which task has the potential to be converted into a project. You need to develop some knack viewing opportunities, gaps and threats as potential projects.

STRATEGY #3: DEVELOP MIX OF PROFESSIONAL AFFILIATIONS

This is one of the easily accessible sources of developing your portfolio. Nature of affiliations will vary from memberships to volunteering, getting involved in a board member of some not-for-profit organizations. Some examples may be:

- **Membership:** Taking up the membership of a couple of really good training or learning related professional bodies is a good idea. You may consider the mix of local, global and remote (online) professional bodies. Choosing a global professional body like ASTD with a local chapter in your metro will be beneficial in the long run in terms of developing contacts, participating in several learning events, networking with other members and potentially striking some collaboration. You may get a chance to volunteer in some of the chapter events and get noticed. If you are resourceful, you may be able to get onto the executive council. That will add to your portfolio of management. If you are building your portfolio for next level role in management, then you better seek membership with institutes, professional bodies, and associations which give you an edge over and above an individual contributor. Examples could be project management, consulting, learning management related organizations.

- **Certification:** Some of the professional bodies have stringent criteria to award the membership (example CIPD) which acts as a certification in itself.

- **Online Groups:** LinkedIn groups may also help you a lot while you are sitting in your home. This is the time for the thought leaders and opinion leaders. LinkedIn groups are a great place to establish your credibility as an influencer and a thought leader. This gives you the opportunity to refine and organize your ideas and opinions before you post it or reply to the ongoing discussion. This is one key skill you may need when you are stepping up to a new management role.

- **Volunteering:** Volunteering for getting involved in events of some organizations like PMI as a volunteer can give you the good experience you are looking for. Taking the initiative to apply for opening a local chapter for a known professional body if the one does not exist in your city will stand you as a leader in your area of expertise. If you are successful in opening the local chapter for a professional organization, it will actually give you superb managerial experience too.

- **Academic service:** Register your profile for becoming a member of the editorial board of journals in your area of expertise. This will equip you with certain best practices which are not even in print yet.

STRATEGY #4: WRITE IN YOUR AREA OF EXPERTISE

Whether or not you have flair for writing, you still may be able to find several avenues matching your skill set. Trainers and instructional designers usually have well-developed writing skills. However, they need to use their writing skills to build their portfolio for next level role.

- **Discussion Forums:** Very basic form of writing may be participating in Q&A as well as online discussion forums. This will not only help you organize your thoughts, opinions and stands but also help you build a noticeable portfolio of influence. Several employers are using your social media presence to assess the level of value you can add to organizations and your professional standing in the community of experts like you.
- **Blog:** Eventually you may want to set up your blogs. WordPress or Blogspot may be a good option for starters. This will help you build your portfolio of online presence and opinions slowly and slowly. Be careful what you write. Once posted on the

internet stays there forever in some shape and form. Your writings will be a reflection of your professional expertise.

* **Articles & books:** If you are good at writing, I suggest writing a few articles in the magazines or online blogs and even posting those on SlideShare kind of open repositories. If you already have written a lot, then why not pull all those together under SlideShare or Selected Works and build your portfolio there? If you are outstanding in writing why not to write a short book?

You might want to play it little strategically. If you are building a portfolio to move into training or learning management role, you better write something about managing certain elements thereof.

STRATEGY #5: GET INVOLVED IN CONSULTING ACTIVITIES

Consulting skill is one of the highly sought after skill in learning and training domain. As you will study the career path of highly successful training consultants, you would know that they were strong individual contributors at one point. The managers in training and learning domains are expected to have good consulting skills given the nature of today's client-oriented training business. Also, managers are expected to be strong consulting leaders for their team to bring new strategies, models, methods and techniques to their companies.

There are some avenues you may be able to get involved in easily and develop your consulting or advisory skills:

- **Volunteer Service:** Join some volunteer training organizations where you can participate in some advisory services free of charge. Some organizations are involved in youth education, adult training, and community enrichment programs.

- **Mentoring and guidance:** Several leading universities and educational institute constantly keep looking for qualified working professionals as a career mentor for their graduates depending upon the credentials. Even the university you graduated from may also have opportunities as alumni. The mentoring usually involves guiding to-be-graduated students for career choice, employment search strategies, project guidance, resume review, and specific guidance based on their specialization. The commitment may range from a few hours a month of commitment to a few days a year of involvement.

- **Free training or consulting sessions:** Deliver some free training sessions to groups you are associated with (like your community club, the organization you volunteer for, your school or even your team). From that point onwards you would see lots of inquiries coming for help. In the beginning, it may find it tiring, but eventually, you would be able to convert these opportunities to polish your consulting skills. There are several agencies out there who would want to sign you when they hear you provide free training and they would want to have you on their rolls of associate trainers or consultant for their clients.

Remember that 'telling is not consulting' and counseling or advising is also not consulting skill. You probably need to deal it quite professionally to develop a refined consulting skill which will give you an edge when you are stepping up for a management role.

TAKE AWAY

You need to deliver with your key expertise otherwise you would get lost in the crowd. One word of caution if you are in a full-time job. You might want to join such activities as not-for-profit so that there is no conflict of interest with your employer. Joining educational and not-for-profit organizations which do not really bring a commercial gain for you would be advisable.

◆ ◆ ◆ ◆ ◆

THE AUTHOR

Raman K Attri is a corporate business researcher, learning strategist, and management consultant with a strong zeal to enable people to unravel human learning and performance. His international professional career spanned over 25 years across a range of disciplines such as scientific research, systems engineering, management consulting, training operations, academic & professional teaching and learning design. He specializes in providing the competitive and strategic value to the organizations by accelerating time-to-proficiency of employees through well-researched models. He holds a doctorate in business from Southern Cross University, Australia. A strong proponent of learning as the core of human success, he provides advisory on accelerated learning techniques which earned him over 60 educational credentials including doctorate degrees, three masters' degrees and tens of international certifications. Despite an unfortunate permanent physically disability since childhood, he leveraged it to learn, research and test a range of "how to methods" to accelerate the rate of personal learning and professional performance at workplace. He has published his methods in scholarly journals, blogs and books and presented at leading international conferences. He also runs a non-profit consulting forum focused on researching and publishing strategies to accelerate speed to proficiency through networked researchers.

INDEX

Speed To Proficiency
RESEARCH

Accelerated Performance for Accelerated Times

Highly-specialized know-how, learning, and resources to solve challenges of 'time' and 'speed' in performance at organizational, professional and personal levels.

Visit us at https://www.speedtoproficiency.com/

S2Pro© Speed To Proficiency Research is a corporate research and consulting forum that provides authentic guidelines to business practitioners to accelerate proficiency of their workforce, teams, and professionals at the 'speed of business'. S2Pro© publishes reports, ebooks, and articles exclusively related to accelerated performance, accelerated proficiency and accelerated expertise in individual and organizational context. Our extensive knowledge base of "how to methods" is derived from experience-based and practice-based observations, analysis/synthesis of existing research, or based on planned/focused research studies through a network of researchers who exclusively focus on 'time' and 'speed' metrics in the business context.

Speed To Proficiency Research: S2Pro©
A research and consulting forum
Singapore 560463

Website: https://www.speedtoproficiency.com
e-mail: rkattri@speedtoproficiency.com
Facebook: https://www.facebook.com/speedtoproficiency/
LinkedIn: https://www.linkedin.com/company/speedtoproficiency/
Twitter: https://www.twitter.com/speed2expertise
Google+: https://plus.google.com/101561704929830160312